Silly Sticker Stories™

Halloween Tales

HIGHLIGHTS PRESS

Honesdale, Pennsylvania

Create your own silly story!

Each Hidden Pictures® puzzle in this book comes with a story for you to finish. Use the tear-out sticker sheets to start puzzling!

Here's what you do:

1 Find a hidden object.

2 Peel the sticker.

Tear out sticker sheet here.

Live from the Monster Olympics
pages 4–5

pennant · bandage · lollipop · flyswatter · sailboat
pizza · straw · hockey stick · flashlight · hat · ghost

Halloween Night
pages 6–7

hockey stick · sailboat · pine tree · ladle · comb · straw · hammer · boot
lemon · shark · flower pot · crown · ice skate

Lost in Transit
pages 8–9

ice-cream cone · top hat · comb · toothbrush · crown · canoe

...ights for Children, Inc.

Live from the Monster Olympics

Welcome to the Monster _____ Network. _____ nsters, all the time. Today, we take you to the biggest _____ in our history. It's the Monster Olympics—sponsored by our friends at Furry _____ Tasty Bites: Put a Tasty Bite in your lunchbox today. We are off to a great start here at Growling _____ Stadium. We've seen Frank. N. _____ win the difficult _____-lifting event and Ima Witch set a record in _____ jumping. Now we head to the volleyball court, where the sand is as soft as a baby werewolf's _____. The local favorite, _____ Wrap from Egypt, is ready to serve the _____. He stretches his _____ and . . . wait a minute! Wrap has stopped to eat a Tasty Bite. It looks as if he hasn't eaten in thousands of years. After this pause in the _____, we'll be right back.

BONUS: Can you find the banana and ice-cream sandwich?

Illustrated by Neil Numberman

4

5

Contents

3

Place it in the story.

4

Read aloud and giggle!

Illustrated by Paula Becker

4

Live from the Monster Olympics

Welcome to the Monster __60__ Network: all monsters, all

the time. Today, we take you to the biggest __sport__ in our

history. It's the Monster Olympics— sponsored by our friends at

Furry __club__ Tasty Bites: Put a Tasty Bite in your lunchbox

today. We are off to a great start here at Growling __GYM__

Stadium. We've seen Frank. N. __El__ win the difficult

__life__-lifting event and Ima Witch set a record in __soccer__

jumping. Now we head to the volleyball court, where the sand

is as soft as a baby werewolf's __arm__. The local favorite,

__sport__ Wrap from Egypt, is ready to serve the __lunch__.

He stretches his __Butt__ and . . . wait a minute! Wrap has

stopped to eat a Tasty Bite. It looks as if he hasn't eaten in thousands

of years. After this pause in the __GYM__, we'll be right back.

BONUS: Can you find the banana and ice-cream sandwich?

Illustrated by Neil Numberman

Halloween Night

Have you ever heard the expression, "Trick or treat, smell my

_____"? I think that's kind of mean. After all, if people are

giving me candy to put in my _____, I want to be as nice to

them as a young _____ to a sweet _____! I'm glad my

friends agree with me. This year my best buddy, Henry, put a squishy

_____ on his head and pretended to be an old _____.

He is hilarious! I decided to wear a green crown and hold a big

_____. Get it? I'm the Statue of _____! Henry and I

and a bunch of friends went trick-or-treating together. I think our

neighbors liked seeing us standing on their _____; especially

Mr. _____. He handed me a sugarcoated _____—my

favorite! I said thanks, and then I ate the whole thing before we got

to the next _____. I mean, that's the polite

thing to do, right?

BONUS: Can you find the fishhook?

Lost in Transit

Last night, I thought I was as lost as a stray _____ in a strange

_____. I flew in circles over the town of West _____

for hours looking for the _____ party I was attending. I was

supposed to be the party's honored _____! But every time I

glanced down from the _____ I was riding on, I could see only

towering _____ trees. Then my cat, Mr. Fuzzy _____

Fluffkins, meowed at me. "Oh, right!" I replied, and grabbed my big

_____ that was hanging nearby. I opened it, pushed aside an

old _____, and grabbed my bewitched _____ phone.

After pressing a few buttons, I was back on track! I found the party

lickety-split. I gave Mr. Fluffkins an extra big helping of ground-up

_____ at the party to say thank you.

BONUS: Can you find the worm,
banana, and fried egg?

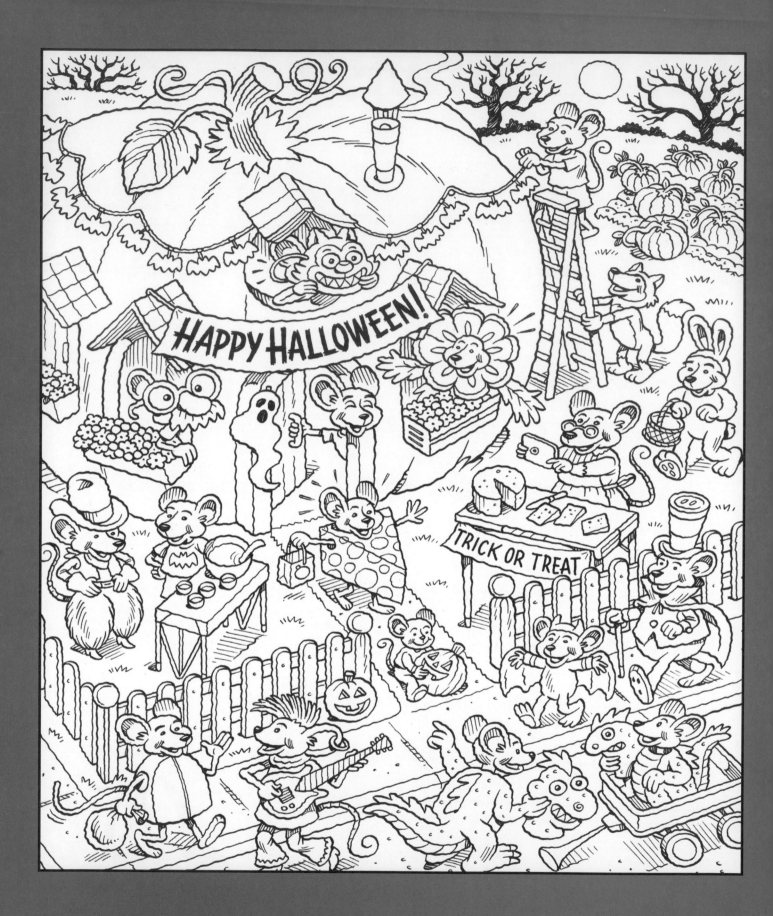

"Trick or Cheese!"

Halloween in Mouseville is anything but boring. First of all, there

is the _____ decorating contest. This year my mom stuck

a chocolate-covered _____ on our front door! Then

there is the neighborhood party, where everyone carves a giant

_____ and then eats a _____ stuffed with apple butter.

But my favorite part of Halloween here is trick-or-treating. My

_____ always gets filled with the best _____ on the

planet. Not only do we get candy, but people also hand out all kinds

of cheese, including my favorite: Swiss _____. This year, I'm

dressing up as Count _____. I bet I'll be the only vampire with

a _____ on his head! My two best buddies are dressing as a

pair of _____ and _____ shakers. We're going to have

more fun than a _____ at a circus! Happy Halloween!

BONUS: Can you find the open book and slice of pie?

Cat Karaoke

Come on down to Cat Karaoke this October. Just like last

month, Deejay "_____ Whiskers" will be playing the best

_____ music to yowl to. That includes the spooky hit song by

The Catnip _____. If you're more in a purring mood, don't

worry, we'll have slow favorites like, "No Furball in My _____"

and "Scratch that _____ Today." The cat with the best

karaoke voice will win a stay at the _____ Hotel, and a new

Ace 100 _____ to keep your claws sharp and shiny. Maybe

eating is more your thing than singing. No purr-blem! There will be

_____-flavored crunchy mice, fish with _____ sauce,

and wild _____ stew. Still on the fence? We've got a brand

new _____ to dance on, too! So wash your whiskers,

put on your fanciest _____, and come on down!

BONUS: Can you find the peanut and arrow?

Illustrated by Paula Becker

Pumpkin Hauling

Every year my family gets in our four-wheel-drive _____ and

heads to Bo's Supersized _____ and Pumpkin Patch. And

every year, I get stuck carrying the heaviest _____. All while

my charming little sister (a.k.a "the little _____") watches me

heave and haul—without even offering to lend a _____. The

other bad thing about Bo's is that there's no squishy _____

to wallow in. It's hard to go so long without rubbing my hoof in

a _____ puddle or at least on a damp _____. But, it

means a lot to Dad to find the perfect _____ for Halloween.

And truthfully, I love a good _____ as much as he does. So I

pick up a giant pumpkin that weighs more than a _____. Then

my sister says to me, "When we get home, you can be first to jump

in the muddy _____." Maybe she isn't so bad after all!

BONUS: Can you find the mushroom, banana, nail,
musical note, wishbone, drinking straw, crescent moon, and candle?

Scared In Transylvania

I am a vampire and Halloween scares me. My brother thinks this

is hilarious. "You'd better get into your _____ and pull the

_____ over your head until November," he says. Nothing

scares him. Not even a black _____ crossing his path while

he walks under a _____! Mom says I need to face my fears.

She is making me decorate the _____ for Halloween. I think

that stinks more than my brother's old _____. We have super

scary _____ decorations—like a coffin with a _____

on it, and a skull with a _____ dripping from its eyes. But I

told Mom I'd try. She says I'm being a good _____. Then Dad

gives me some advice. "When you see a scary _____, picture

it wearing a clown's nose." I picture a giant _____ clown and

giggle. Maybe I can get through Halloween after all!

BONUS: Can you find
the baseball cap, slice of pie, and heart?

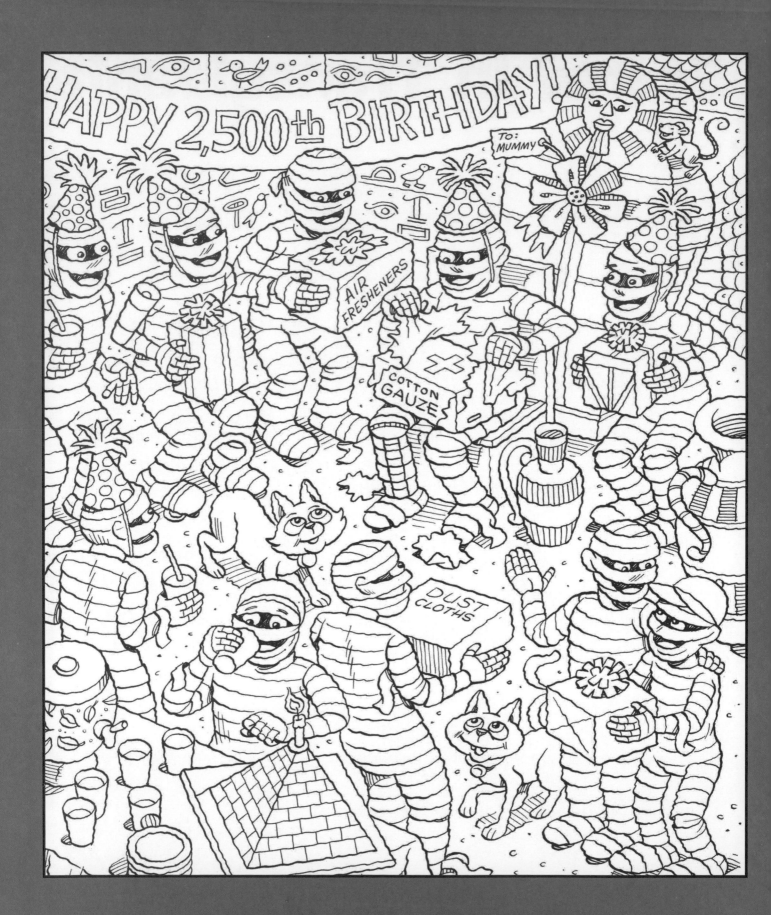

A Special Birthday

"Happy _____ Day to me! I'm an ancient mummy!" That's

my favorite song. I sing it every year on October 31st—my birthday.

That's when my friends throw me a big _____ party, complete

with cake made from a tasty _____, a punch bowl filled with

a _____ and dry ice, and a mound of gifts. We mummies

know how to party! Before I open my first _____, everyone

hits the dance floor. I do the _____ Boogie. When my favorite

song, "Wrap It Up," comes on, I jump up onto the _____ and

show my best moves. Luckily I don't squish the _____ on the

food tray. After that, I need a break. I open my gifts and unwrap

a ticket to ride a _____ all the way to the North Pole! I've

always wanted to see a _____ bear. My friends even got me

a warm new _____ to wear on my trip. I sure am a lucky

_____!

BONUS: Can you find the banana,
screw, bowl, and leaf?

Illustrated by David Helton

A Monster Sale

Halloween is two days away, and I still need a costume. I want to

dress up like a _____ chief. My little sister thinks being a fairy

_____ would be more fun. I was planning to make my own

costume out of a cardboard _____, a flashing _____,

and a hard plastic _____. But just try to find all that in our

house—no way. Luckily, Dad heard about a new _____ shop

nearby that's having a sale on costumes. We all piled in the family's

_____ and headed there. The store is fantastic! Right away, I

found the _____ I'd been trying to find. But as I watched my

sister prance around with a _____ on her head, I got an idea.

If I wrapped a _____ around my shoulders, my sister and I

could be a really funny _____ set. I asked her, and she

said, "_____!" I can't wait to go trick-or-treating!

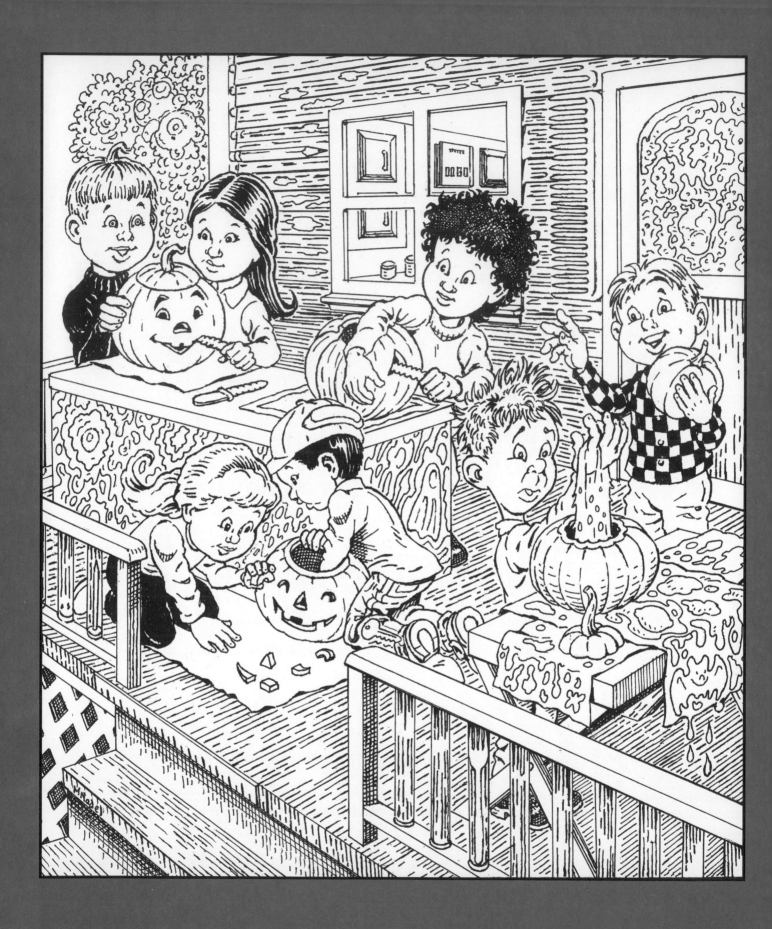

Goopy Scoops

The big day is here! The annual neighborhood _____-carving

contest. I was so excited last night that I tossed and turned on

my _____ for hours. I have big plans. I want to turn my

pumpkin into a replica of a _____. Won't that be spooky?! So

today, I used a safety _____ and cut the top off of the best

_____ I could find. Then I stuck my hand in and scooped out

a giant glob of _____. Ew, it was slimy. I kept on scooping

until I had a pile as tall as a _____. But I still hadn't scraped

every _____ out. I looked around. The girl next to me was

holding a _____ and had started carving. I felt as frustrated

as a _____. That's when a kid handed me a special curved

_____. "It makes the scooping go faster," he said. Did it ever!

Finally, I'm ready to carve. Maybe I'll win first _____ this year!

BONUS: Can you find the bat, chick, and hot dog?

Illustrated by Marc Nadel

23

Ghostly Games

I have a new favorite game. It's called "Ghosts in the _____."

Of course, I love it. I am a _____, after all. The rules are

pretty simple. Someone is "it" and covers his or her _____

with a _____. Everyone else hides. They can scrunch down

behind a _____ or even climb up a _____. Then the

_____ who is "it," tries to find everyone. You probably know

this game as "Hide and _____." Whatever you call it, it's

tons of fun. Tonight's game was epic. My best _____, Gertie,

was "it." Instead of searching for the rest of us, she lay down on a

_____ and closed her eyes. Soon, she was snoring as loud as

a raging _____. The rest of us couldn't believe it. We figured

it was safe to come out. But when we did, Gertie yelled, "Awesome

_____!" and tagged us all.

BONUS: Can you find the tooth
and the snake?

Illustrated by Paula Becker

Cauldron Contest

This is a witch's favorite time of year. The time when she can

pull out her biggest _____ from storage and fill it with

goodies—things like a slice of rotten _____, one giant oozing

_____, and essence of _____. This year, Halloween

Town is having a fun _____ cooking contest. The only rule

is that the judge, Ms. _____ Cackle, has to taste a pinch

of _____ in each cauldron. Sounds easy, right? But that

ingredient hasn't been seen in town for months. Not since an angry

_____ stole the last bag of it. Thankfully, a young witch named

Wanda _____ followed the thief and saw him hide the bag

in an old _____. The night before the contest, Wanda put

on a warm _____ and scurried off with a bag of her own.

She found the secret stash and brought some to each _____

in town. The next day, Wanda won "Worst Batch"—that is witch

language for first place!

BONUS: Can you find the ice-cream bar,
present, and bird?

Illustrated by Susan T. Hall

The Spooky Salon

Don't let your fur, hair, or _____ look unruly on Halloween.

Grab your _____ and get down to Hair Today right now. We

are having a gruesome sale on _____ waxing and trimming.

One _____ for the price of two! Ha! Just kidding. We'll give

you ten. Remember, we use only the most spoiled ingredients in our

patented "Ugly _____ Lotion." It just costs one _____!

You'll look worse after only one use—we guarantee it. And we

know you'll want to smell your nastiest for _____-or-treating,

so our special perfume, Odor of _____, is half off! It also

doubles as food for your pet _____. Yes, there's nothing

like Hair Today for the holiday. We are on the corner of Smelly

_____ Avenue and Old _____ Street. Every monster

wants the very best for themselves. You won't find that here—but

we will give you a free furry _____ with every visit.

BONUS: Can you find the ice-cream cone and shuttlecock?

Happy Hauntings

"We wish you a merry _____!" OK, I know you usually sing

that song in December as a Christmas _____. But October

31st is my favorite _____ ever, so I changed the words.

I'm going trick-or-treating with my friends tonight. I hope I get a

chocolate-covered _____"—that's my favorite—and a salted-

caramel _____. I wouldn't even mind putting my teeth into

a sour _____. I don't know what to expect from our new

neighbors. They moved into the huge old _____ down the

street from us. When I was a little _____, I thought it was

haunted. No one has lived there for years. Until now. I felt a little

nervous walking up the _____ to the house. When I stepped

on a _____, I nearly jumped a foot high. But when I rang

the door _____, a very nice _____ came to the door.

Whew. Nothing spooky here! Merry Halloween to you!

BONUS: Can you find the tack, needle, sock, and banana?

Illustrated by Michael Palan

A Ghostly Outing

I am a ghost, and this is the first year I'm allowed to go trick-or-

treating. Mom has always said, "You are a _____, son. You

aren't supposed to go trick-or-treating. You are supposed to be

spooky and frighten every _____ on the street and each

_____ in the yard." "But, mom," I'd whine, "I want to eat a

_____ like every other kid!" So finally, she gave in. I'm about

to ring my first _____. I can hear someone coming to the

_____ right now. As the doorknob turns, I shout, "Trick

or _____!" And then I scream for real. What I see is more

frightening than a _____ wearing a clean _____! But

then I see that the creature is scared of me, too. I force myself to

stand still and hold out my _____. "Er, _____ or treat?"

I ask quietly. The creature plops a _____ in my basket. We

smile at each other. I can't wait to see what the next house brings!

BONUS: Can you find the carrot?

Perfect Party

Each Halloween my cousin Amanda throws a big _____ party.

It is the best! We play pin the _____ on the _____.

We have a _____-eating contest. And of course, we do the

_____ dance. But my favorite part is that everyone gets

to carve a _____. This year, I want to give mine a face like

my pet _____. It will be super cute! But when I arrive at

Amanda's, I see that the party room is already full of carved jack-o'-

lanterns. "_____!" I say under my breath. I feel disappointed,

but I try not to let Amanda know. So I put a _____ on my

face and join in the fun. But Amanda knows me too well. "What's

the _____?" she asks. When I tell her the truth, she smiles.

"Don't worry!" she says. "There are lots more to carve out in the

back _____." Yes! I give her a high-five and race out back. Like

I said, there's no better _____ than Amanda's.

BONUS: Can you find the banana, and envelope?

Illustrated by Dana Regan

Monster Town News

It was a dark and stormy _____. Perfect for Halloween. If

only all the news were so good. Here on Channel _____,

we just found out that there has been a candy burglary at Crystal's

_____ Shop, the biggest candy store in Monster Town!

The creepy crooks got away with every chocolate _____

bar, every piece of _____ gum, and every sugarcoated

_____. Who could do such an unsweet thing? I'll tell you

who: that crusty villain, Cheesy Mc_____. He's been angry

ever since Crystal stopped selling his cheddar-covered _____

bites. But she had no choice: they were infested with those nasty

_____ beetles! I bet it was him. Hold on, this just came in

over the MonsterNet: Crystal found the missing _____! Turns

out, she forgot she had donated it to the town's Halloween party.

Well, all's well that ends well. Now, let's look at that _____

forecast again.

BONUS: Can you find the screw?

Illustrated by Neil Numberman

Witch Cookies?

My family is proof that even witches like to bake from scratch.

We don't just point a magic _____ at a pan and expect a

perfect buttery _____ to pop out. Nope, we enjoy mixing

each cup of _____ and every teaspoon of _____ to

create our special Halloween _____ cookies. I confess—we

do use a little magic. Like tonight—my aunt suggested we hold a

contest to see who could get their _____ to hover in the air

the longest. It came down to my little brother, _____ Jr., and

our mom. Mom was so close, but then her _____ cookie

plopped onto our furry pet _____. My brother got to fly

around the _____ as his prize. Lucky him! I'm not too jealous,

though. Tonight is Halloween, which means I get to fly up to the

_____ and back on my brand new _____. Lucky me!

BONUS: Can you find the banana and envelope?

Confessions of a Dog

Everyone in my family seems to think that Purrkins the Cat painted

the "Mona _____" and climbed Mount _____—all in

the same day. Sure, she's cute. But dogs—like me—deserve more

respect. Specifically, I deserve a giant _____ covered with

cheese to eat, a soft fuzzy _____ to sleep on, and more

scratches on the top of my _____. But what do I get? My

owner Katy carving a giant _____ into a mirror image of

Purrkins! I'm so angry I could dig a hole in the _____ garden.

That would prove who's the better _____! Now, here comes

Katy's brother carrying a big _____. Is he going to carve

another _____ of Purrkins?! Yup, he just carved a floppy . . .

Wait. Hold on. That looks like my _____. Could it be?! YES! It

is a hot-diggity _____ pumpkin! Like I always say, "Dogs rule.

Cats drool." Except Purrkins. I confess, I kind of like that kitty.

BONUS: Can you find the eyeglasses and wedge of lemon?

Illustrated by Jennifer Zivoin

41

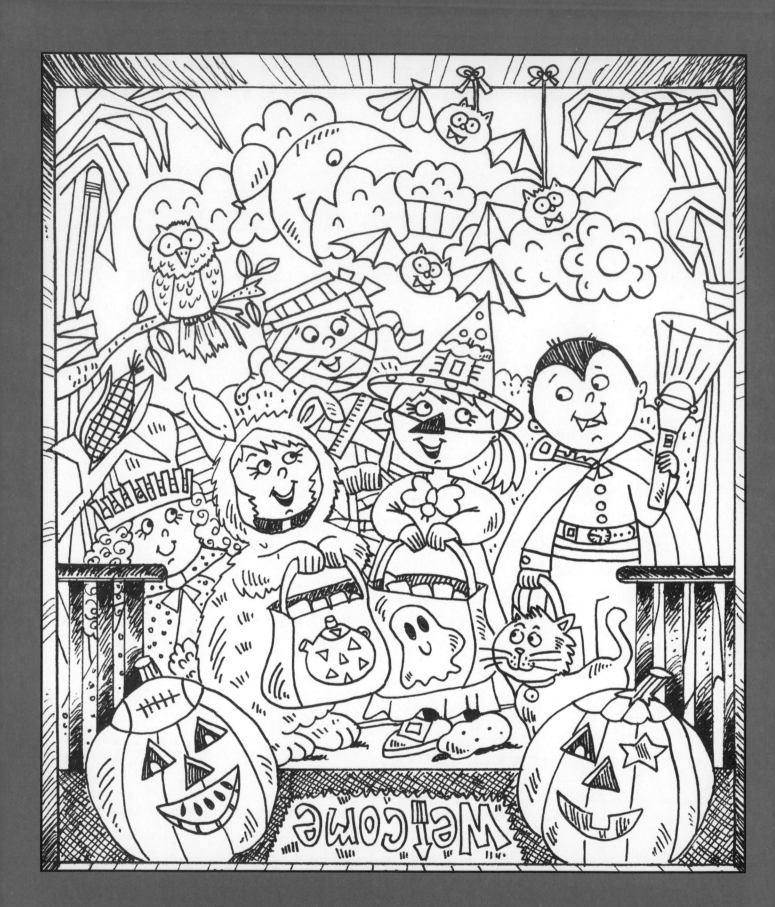

Halloween Camp

I had never heard of Halloween Camp before this summer. Dad

signed me up for a week in July. I was nervous. Would I find

another _____ to talk to? Would I sleep OK on a strange

_____? And would they have my favorite food, mac-

and-_____? It turned out, I didn't need to worry. Camp

was great! We worked all week to create our own _____

to wear trick-or-treating. Then on the last day, we each grabbed

a _____ to put candy in, and we knocked on every

_____ at the camp. Counselors gave us a lot of sweet

_____ bars. Then we went back to the main _____ and

had a Halloween party. There were games, like _____ tag,

and tons of crafts to make. I created a _____ out of dried-up

_____ chips! I traded it with a friend for his _____ mask

made from canned pumpkin. It was a happy, hot Halloween!

BONUS: Can you find the worm, muffin, screwdriver, ruler, star, flower,
slice of watermelon, potato, pencil, and seashell?

Illustrated by Mernie Gallagher Cole

The Monster 5-K

It's Halloween day and every ghoul and _____ in town is over

at Grizzly _____ Park for the annual 5-K race. The K stands for

"Kooky." Each year, the town holds a contest to find the five kookiest

monsters to run along the dirt _____ through the deep, dark

_____. This year's racers include a witch flying on a brown

_____ and a young werewolf with only one _____ on her

left foot! The whole town comes out to cheer. Lots of us volunteer

to hand out _____ bottles to runners—it's important to stay

hydrated with plenty of ice-cold _____ during a race. This year's

grand prize is a meal at The Cackling _____ Cafeteria. Who

wouldn't want that?! I am rooting for my best _____, Belinda

Bat. But no matter who comes in first _____, all five are already

winners. They are the kookiest monsters in _____ Town, after

all. Happy Halloween to everyone!

Answers

▼ Front Cover

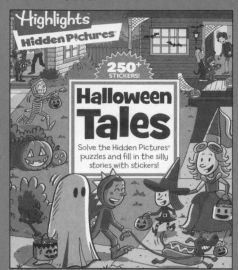

▼ Page 4

▼ Page 6

▼ Page 8

▼ Page 10

▼ Page 12

▼ Page 14

▼ Page 16

▼ Page 18

Answers

▼ Page 20

▼ Page 22

▼ Page 24

▼ Page 26

▼ Page 28

▼ Page 30

▼ Page 32

▼ Page 34

▼ Page 36

Answers

▼Page 38

▼Page 40

▼Page 42

▼Page 44

Live from the Monster Olympics
pages 4–5

bandage

lollipop

flyswatter

sailboat

ghost

hat

pennant

pizza

straw

hockey stick

flashlight

boot

Halloween Night
pages 6–7

ladle

comb

straw

hammer

ice skate

hockey stick

sailboat

pine tree

lemon

shark

flower pot

crown

Lost in Transit
pages 8–9

comb

toothbrush

canoe

pizza

sock

ice-cream cone

top hat

ruler

lime

crown

fish

hamburger

"Trick or Cheese!"
pages 10–11

spatula

lollipop

necklace

toothbrush

button

necktie

crown

flashlight

golf tee

chili pepper

golf club

sailboat

Cat Karaoke
pages 12–13

teardrop

worm

spoon

fish

pizza

dog bone

wishbone

toothbrush

baseball

cupcake

envelope

flashlight

Pumpkin Hauling
pages 14–15

baseball cap

pencil

shoe

bell

ruler

mitten

comb

pail

button

paintbrush

sock

fish

Scared in Transylvania
pages 16–17

spoon

bugle

hammer

horseshoe

baseball bat

bird

fishhook

carrot

kite

book

ring

toothbrush

A Special Birthday
pages 18–19

crown · saltshaker · pennant · key · kite · pizza · bow tie · flashlight · sailboat · ring · crescent moon

A Monster Sale
pages 20–21

bacon · lollipop · ring · snake · pencil · banana · snow cone · chili pepper · ladle · pennant · cupcake · mug · thread

Goopy Scoops
pages 22–23

magnet · lemon · comb · ruler · swim fin · key · teddy bear · pencil · nail · book · fried egg · fork

Ghostly Games
pages 24–25

glove · mushroom · sock · domino · spoon · baseball bat · football · comb · yo-yo · cactus · bowl · paintbrush

Cauldron Contest
pages 26–27

ladder · ice-cream cone · candle · bread · ring · truck · snowman · mitten · teacup · saucepan · crayon · umbrella

The Spooky Salon
pages 28–29

tweezers · fork · canoe · acorn · ladybug · wrench · light bulb · safety pin · tent · hammer · necktie · saltshaker

Happy Haunting
pages 30–31

paintbrush · ladder · spoon · fish · drumstick · teapot · pizza · hanger · toothbrush · flashlight · toothpaste · slipper

Highlights™ Highlights™

Hidden Pictures® Hidden Pictures®

Highlights™ Highlights™

Hidden Pictures® Hidden Pictures®

Highlights™ Highlights™

Hidden Pictures® Hidden Pictures®

Highlights™ Highlights™

Hidden Pictures® Hidden Pictures®

Highlights™ Highlights™

Hidden Pictures® Hidden Pictures®

Highlights™ Highlights™

Hidden Pictures® Hidden Pictures®

Highlights™ Highlights™

A Ghostly Outing
pages 32–33

megaphone · crescent moon · pencil · pizza · glove · flashlight · toothbrush

fork · sock · ruler · yo-yo · fish

Perfect Party
pages 34–35

goggles · green bean · French fry · pennant · comb

fish · cheese · pie · domino · hockey stick · cinnamon bun · toothbrush

Monster Town News
pages 36–37

snake · book · domino · hockey stick

spatula

megaphone · pitcher · matchstick · lollipop · pie · pizza · ruler

Witch Cookies
pages 38–39

paintbrush · golf club · thread · mitten · button

feather · pennant · flashlight · pie · horseshoe · ice-cream bar · iron

Confessions of a Dog
pages 40–41

magnifying glass · pear · boot · baseball · pinecone

golf tee · turtle · iron · crayon · coin purse · clothespin · fish

Halloween Camp
pages 42–43

wristwatch · comb · key · ladder · pizza

fish · balloon · pail · butterfly · teapot · football · feather

The Monster 5-K
pages 44–45

worm · flashlight · lightning bolt · heart · apple

pizza · cupcake · dustpan · flag · crown · ruler · needle